TURKEY AND ISTANBUL

PHILIP STEELE

W

FRANKLIN WATTS
LONDON•SYDNEY

DEVELOPING WORLD

TURKEY AND ISTANBUL

W
FRANKLIN WATTS
LONDON•SYDNEY

First published in 2014 by
Franklin Watts
338 Euston Road
London
NW1 3BH

Franklin Watts Australia
Level 17/207 Kent Street
Sydney
NSW 2000

HB ISBN 978 1 4451 2363 9
eBook ISBN 978 14451 2369 1

Dewey number: 914.961/915.61

A CIP catalogue record for this book is
available from the British Library.

Series Editor: Julia Bird
Series Advisor: Emma Epsley, geography teacher and consultant
Series Design: sprout.uk.com

Picture credits:
AFP/Getty Images: 9. Walter Allgower/Alamy: 13. Adem Altan/AFP/Getty Images: 10, 29b.
Angelmaker/Dreamstime: 19t. Archives du 7e Art Zeynofilm/Photos12/Alamy: 35t.
Bart Pro/Alamy: 18b. Tibor Bognar/Alamy: 42. Orhan Cam/Shutterstock: 12.
Caro/Alamy: 16, 40. Mehmet Cetin/Shutterstock: 6. Mike Cohen/Shutterstock: 34.
Kobby Dagan/Dreamstime: 22. Elfred/Shutterstock: 43b. Faraways/Shutterstock: 28, 32.
Jeremy Graham/Alamy: 14t. Sadic Gulec/Shutterstock: 11b, 14b, 25b, 43t. Haytham Pictures/Alamy: 41b.
Images & Stories/Alamy: 39b. Mykola Irashchenko/Shutterstock: 27. Svetlana Jafarova/Shutterstock: 18t.
JM Travel Photography/Shutterstock: 21t. Kevin Landwer-Johan/istockphoto: 39r. Evren Kalinbacak/Shutterstock: 25t, 38.
Timothy Large /Shutterstock: 21b. Lonely Planet Images/Getty Images: 24b. LOOK Die Bildagentur der Fotografen GmbH/
Alamy: 19bl. Viacheslav Lopatin/Shutterstock: 15t. Tina Lorien/istockphoto: 33b. mehmetcan/Shutterstock: 37.
Melis/Shutterstock: 35b. Muratart/Shutterstock: 24t. Alexander Nemenov/Getty Images: 26b.
Ho New/Reuters: 31b. nexus7/Shutterstock: front cover b, 3b, 15br. 1001nights/istockphoto: 26t.
Petitfrere/Dreamstime: 17t, Paul Prescott/Shutterstock: 31t. Red Diplomat/istockphoto: 19br.
Joe Restuccia III/Alamy: 23b. Pascal Saez/Alamy: 36t. Alex Segre/Alamy: 39tl. Valery Shanin/Shutterstock: 20.
Alexey Stoganov/istockphoto: 17b. Boris Stroujko/Shutterstock: 23t. David Sutherland/Alamy: 11t.
Marco Tomasini/Shutterstock: 36b. Alexander A Trofimov//Shutterstock: 33t. Typhoonski/Dreamstime: front cover t, 3t.
Martyn Unsworth/Dreamstime: 7c. Paul Vinten/Shutterstock: 15bl. Janine Wiedel/Photolibrary/Alamy: 30.

Printed in Malaysia

Franklin Watts is a division of
Hachette Children's Books,
an Hachette UK company.
www.hachette.co.uk

TURKEY AND ISTANBUL

CONTENTS

EAST MEETS WEST

BRIDGING THE BOSPHORUS

On one side is Europe. On the other is Asia. Between these two continents lies a narrow strip of blue sea. This is the Bosphorus, 31 kilometres in length and just 0.4 to 1.8 kilometres across. The Bosphorus strait links the Black Sea with the Sea of Marmara, and its gateway is Istanbul, Turkey's largest city. For thousands of years passengers could only cross the Bosphorus by boat, but today two great suspension bridges span it, and a third one is under construction. Times are changing in Turkey.

WELCOME TO TURKEY

European Turkey is made up of a small corner of land, known as Eastern Thrace (Doğu Trakya) and bordered by Greece and Bulgaria. The great bulk of Turkey – about 97 per cent of the total area – lies in Asia, where the Anatolia region (Anadolu) stretches eastwards towards Georgia, Armenia, Iran, Iraq and Syria. This is a land of hot summers. Winters are mild along the coasts, but can be bitterly cold in the interior. There are mountains, windswept plateaus and long coastlines. There is also the constant risk of earthquakes – Turkey lies over an active geological area.

The Fatih Sultan Mehmet bridge crosses the Bosphorus strait. It links the European and Asian sides of the city and during rush hour is busy with commuter traffic.

UKRAINE

BULGARIA

Black Sea

GEORGIA

AZERBAIJAN

THRACE

Edirne

Bosphorus

REECE

Istanbul

Sea of Marmara Izmit

Samsun

PONTIC MTS

ARMENIA

Bursa

Adapazan

Ankara

TURKEY

River Euphrates

Erzurum

Eskişehir

ARARAT (5,137m)

Aegean Sea

A N A T O L I A

River Kızılırmak

Izmir

Kayseri

Malatya

Diyarbak

River Tigris

IRAN

Denizil

Konya

CAPPADOCIA

Adana

Gaziantep

TAURUS MTS   Mersin

IRAQ

Antakya

SYRIA

CYPRUS

Dawn lights up the ancient rock citadel of Üçhisar, the highest point in Cappadocia.

Mediterranean Sea   LEBANON

NEW DIRECTIONS

Turkey's economy has been racing ahead. Some experts say that by 2023 it could be among the world's top ten. Other economists believe that problems may lie ahead. All sorts of political questions are also being asked. Just what kind of country is Turkey turning into? Will Turkey's new-found wealth benefit the poor as well as the rich? What kind of nation is this new Turkey?

Is it a religious, Islamic country or a secular one, in which faith and politics are kept apart? Is it a country which respects the human rights of its minority peoples? What part will Turkey play in the turbulent politics of the Middle East region as a whole? Will it become a member of the European Union (EU) as planned? As it straddles the Bosphorus, should Turkey be looking eastwards into Asia or westwards into Europe? Or should Turkey be acting as bridge builder between the two?

SPOTLIGHT ON TURKEY

FULL NAME: Republic of Turkey • AREA: 783,562 km²
POPULATION: 80,694,485 • CAPITAL: Ankara
(pop. 4.3 million) • BIGGEST CITY: Istanbul
(pop.13.9 million) • LONGEST RIVER: Kızılırmak
(1,355 km) HIGHEST MOUNTAIN: Ağrı (Ararat;
5,137 m) RESOURCES: Bauxite, chromite, copper, iron ore, coal, oil, natural gas, boron salts

A RICH HISTORY

Ottoman troops invaded Europe, besieging Vienna in 1529 and 1683. This old painting shows them capturing a Hungarian town in 1543.

ANCIENT LANDS

In the rocks and dusty soil of Turkey lie the remains of ancient civilisations. Anatolia (see page 6) played an important part in the early development of farming, town building and iron working. In the west and along the Aegean coast are the ruins of ancient Troy and fine cities of the classical world. Byzantium, an ancient Greek settlement on the Bosphorus, became the eastern capital of the Roman Empire in 330 CE. The city blossomed as Constantinople, capital of the medieval Byzantine Empire and a centre of Christianity. Trade brought the riches of Asia through its ports.

TURKISH SULTANS

Turkish peoples originally came from Central Asia. Many invaded the Middle East in the Middle Ages (5–15th centuries CE) and adopted the Muslim faith. One group of Turks, the Seljuks, advanced from Persia (Iran) into Anatolia. They were followed by another group known as the Osmanli or Ottomans, who captured Constantinople in 1453. The city became known as Istanbul, from the Greek words for 'in the city'. Beautiful mosques were built and Turkish sultans ruled in splendour from their palace beside the Bosphorus. Their empire extended across the Middle East, North Africa, Greece and southeastern Europe.

DECLINE AND FALL

Ottoman power declined as Western European nations became ever more powerful. In 1914 the Ottoman Empire entered the First World War on the side of Germany, hoping to win back lost territories. By 1918 it had lost everything. The winners carved up the former empire and a Greek invasion sparked off a bitter war of independence. The last sultan, Mehmet VI, was overthrown in 1922.

A NEW REPUBLIC

In 1923 the capital was moved to Ankara, more centrally located in Anatolia. A new Turkish republic was founded and its first president was an army officer called Mustafa Kemal, known as Atatürk ('Father of the Turks'). Atatürk was an authoritarian leader, a stern nationalist. Cutting all ties with the past, he brought in reforms to create a secular, modern European-style state. He died in 1938, but his Republican People's Party (CHP) continued to rule until 1950 when the country's first democratic election handed power to the right-wing Democratic Party. The Turkish military repeatedly intervened in politics – in 1960, 1971 and again in 1980. Democracy returned to Turkey in 1983, with struggles between left and right, widespread corruption but an improving, developing economy.

Mustafa Kemal Atatürk was the founder of modern Turkey. Masks of his face are being worn here to mark the anniversary of his death.

PEOPLES AND LANGUAGES

GROWING FAST

Nearly 81 million people live in Turkey. The population is growing each year at a rate of about 1.2 per cent, higher than in most of Europe, and the effects of this are felt chiefly around the big cities of Istanbul and Ankara, as well as in coastal areas.

MEET THE TURKS

Around three-quarters of the population are ethnic Turks. Many are descendants of the Turks who settled here in the Middle Ages, and are very proud of their history, culture and identity. Related Turkic peoples live across Central Asia, Russia and China. The Turkish language, *Türkçe*, is spoken throughout the country and has official status.

OTHER CITIZENS

There are about 22 other ethnic groups living in Turkey. For much of its history Turkey has tried to make sure that these citizens see themselves as Turks above all else, with governments suppressing minority cultures. Today steps are being taken to improve minority relations. Some Turkish citizens, such as Greeks and Armenians, belong to peoples who have historic grievances with the Turks. Armenians revolted against Ottoman rule from the 1890s and between 1915 and 1923 over a million of them were massacred by the Turks. Turkish governments have repeatedly rejected accusations that this was genocide.

Young women wave Turkey's national flag at a rally to mark National Youth and Sports Day.

A QUESTION OF DRESS

Beautiful traditional costumes may be worn at regional and historical festivals, but generally Turkish people wear typical European dress. About half of women may also wear the *tesettür*, a simple headscarf or hijab, according to Islamic beliefs about modesty. The wearing of head coverings and full veils in schools and other public buildings was forbidden by Atatürk's secular reforms, but in 2012 the classroom ban on headscarves was lifted. This was very controversial, and the issue is still the subject of intense debate for political as well as religious reasons.

A protest in Istanbul commemorates the bombing of Kurds by Turkish airforce jets at Uludere in 2011. Most of the 34 dead were unarmed teenagers.

PEACE FOR THE KURDS?

The Kurdish people live in Turkey, Syria, Iraq and Iran. Their wish for self-government has led to many years of conflict. In Turkey, Kurds make up about 18 per cent of the population. They mostly live in the mountainous east and speak dialects of the Kurdish language. Over the ages Kurdish identity and language have been suppressed, leading to protests and the formation of pro-Kurdish political parties, some peaceful and some violent. An armed rising began in 1984, dominated by the PKK (Kurdistan Workers' Party). Decades of bombings and attacks by the rebels were met by fierce reprisals, discrimination and human rights abuses. Tens of thousands died and hundreds of thousands were made homeless. In 2013 Abdullah Ocalan, the jailed PKK leader, declared a ceasefire, a breakthrough which suggest both sides are now searching for peace.

ANKARA POLITICS

CENTRE OF GOVERNMENT

Turkey today is a democratic republic, in which people can vote from the age of 18. It is divided into 81 provinces (*iller*). The national capital is the city of Ankara, which is also the centre of government.

A NEW SYSTEM?

The legal framework for running a nation is called the constitution, and in Turkey at the moment it is all up for change. Until now the president has been head of state, appointing a prime minister to run the government. The president elected in 2007 was Abdullah Gül, while the prime minister since 2003 has been Recep Tayyip Erdoğan. In 2012 Erdoğan proposed revising the constitution to give the presidency executive powers and allow him to run for this new office in 2014. These changes have been fiercely opposed by critics, who complain that it is a grab for power. Erdoğan's supporters say he is modernising the system.

ELECTION TIME

Turkey's next general election is in 2015. The parliament or *Meclis* is called the Grand National Assembly. It has a single chamber with 550 seats. Turkey has no fewer than 61 political parties at the current count. Erdoğan's AKP (Justice & Development Party) is conservative, favouring the 'free market' and moderate Islamic values. The second biggest party, the CHP (Republican People's Party), is social democratic, secular and Kemalist. Smaller parties include far right nationalists, pro-Kurdish parties, socialists, communists, liberals and Greens.

Ankara is Turkey's capital, its seat of government and the second largest city after Istanbul.

HerşeyTÜRKİYEiçin!

WHAT'S THE AGENDA?

More than any other, it is Prime Minister Erdoğan who has shaped the new Turkey. What impact have his policies had? The economy has grown dramatically, although many people remain poor. Progress towards becoming a full member of the European Union (EU) has been unsteady, but having to meet the conditions for EU membership has improved Turkey's human rights record in some areas, if not in others. At times

Erdoğan's AKP has clashed head on with the military, accusing them of plotting yet another takeover. These charges have been rejected by the army and their supporters, who see themselves as guardians of a secular future. Erdoğan's proposed changes to the constitution have stirred up another hornet's nest, but with three terms in office there is little doubt that he is not only controversial, but also an effective politician with an instinct for survival.

Banners proclaim Erdoğan's popularity, but dramatic protests in Istanbul in the summer of 2013 showed that many Turks mistrust his desire for more power and his hardline tactics.

13

FOCUS ON: ISTANBUL

THE GREAT CITY

This city has had many names in its history – Byzantium, Constantinople, Istanbul. The same conditions that brought it success in ancient times still make it great today. Its geographical position places it at a crossroads of trading routes, communications and cultures. Ankara may have taken away its status as capital, but Istanbul remains at the commercial and cultural heart of Turkey.

The wider urban area is now vast, covering 5,343 square kilometres with a population of around 13.9 million. That is an increase of ten times since the 1950s, just one example of the many changes sweeping across Turkey.

HEART OF THE CITY

Istanbul rises from the sea, with an inlet called the Golden Horn forming a natural harbour. Roman and Byzantine ruins can still be seen, and the stone minarets of Ottoman mosques soar above the skyline. But Istanbul is no mere museum; it is full of life. The city dwellers (known as *Stamboullou*) shop, chat, buy and sell. The sounds of the city echo around the streets – traffic, car horns, music, loudspeakers calling faithful Muslims to prayer five times daily. Tourists take boat trips, throng the restaurants around Taksim Square or dance at the night clubs of Beyoğlu.

What is the fuel that keeps Istanbul going? Çay – sweet black tea, served in a small glass. It oils every business deal, every commercial transaction, every social occasion.

Nearly 1,500 years old, the impressive Christian church of Hagia Sophia ('Holy Wisdom') later became a mosque and is now a museum.

The Galata Bridge crosses the Golden Horn, linking the old city district of Sultanahmet with the Karaköy district, known for its shops, markets and restaurants.

A symbol of change, the Sapphire building in Istanbul's Levent district is one of the tallest buildings in Turkey. It includes shops and luxury flats.

The multi-domed Sultanahmet Camii is known as the Blue Mosque in English because of the beautiful blue ceiling tiles inside. Its minarets look out over the Bosphorus.

WORK AND INDUSTRY

ON THE UP?

Turkey is emerging as a big player in world economics. In 2011 its growth rate hit 8.5 per cent, making it the fastest developing nation in Europe. In 2012 the rate dropped to about 3 per cent, but even this lower figure was better than in Europe's more developed nations, where financial crises brought growth to a near standstill. Forecasts for 2013 and 2014 were from 3 to 3.8 per cent. Whether Turkey's success is sustainable in the longer term, however, remains to be seen.

DOING BUSINESS

Almost half of Turkish workers are employed in service industries. There is a strong banking and financial sector, and a successful tourist industry. The manufacturing sector provides jobs for 26 per cent of the workforce. Turkish workers produce household appliances, electronic equipment, cars, ships, garments and textiles and food products such as olive oil. Turkey's trading partners include Germany and other EU countries, Russia, Iraq, Iran and China.

Stock exchange traders wheel and deal in Istanbul. In 2013 all Turkish exchanges were brought together under a single corporation, called Borsa Istanbul.

TAKE-HOME WAGES

The Turkish currency is called the lira and is worth about £0.36p. So how much do people in Turkey earn? The legal minimum wage from 2013 is 804 lira (£293) per month. The Turkish trade unions point out that this is well below what they regard as a living wage. The average income in Turkey after tax is 1,410 lira per month (£513), and that would be the typical payment to a teacher, for example, before overtime is added on. A labourer or cleaner might make 1,200 lira (£430), while management pay scales are more like those in other European countries.

From tree to production line... Workers process olives at a factory in Akhisar, in the Aegean region.

RESOURCES

Turkey is number ten in the world for mineral resources, having reserves of most major metals. There is oil and natural gas too, but Turkey still has to import more of these fuels to meet its needs. Pipelines link Turkey with Azerbaijan, Russia and Iran. A proposed extension may soon be carrying gas westwards to Austria as well.

WIN OR LOSE?

Erdoğan has introduced capitalist, free market economic policies, with many state-run enterprises such as power plants being privatised. Such policies have delivered wealth and growth, but at the same time have increased the gap between rich and poor. There is a gender gap, too. Across the EU, about 65 per cent of women are in work, but in Turkey it is only 25 per cent, and many of those are in low paid jobs.

An international tour guide addresses her customers. Erdoğan has urged women to have more babies, which of course limits their working opportunities.

FOCUS ON: ISTANBUL

MARKET PLACE

The old way of doing business in Istanbul can be seen at its Grand Bazaar or Kapalı Çarşı, the biggest market of its kind in the world, with 61 covered streets and around 4,000 shops, cafés and banks. Street names still show how merchants were grouped together by their trade. Today the bazaar still looks like a treasure house of gleaming copper, oriental carpets, jewellery and cloth, and draws in millions of tourists.

MONEY MAKER

Istanbul has always been about making money, and today this city alone produces over 27 per cent of Turkey's gross domestic product (GDP). It is the financial capital and is home to the headquarters of Turkish and international banks and corporations. The chief business districts are Levent and Maslak. Outer districts are industrial, processing food or producing textiles, electronics and petrochemicals.

PEOPLE AT WORK

Over half of Istanbul's labour force work in services, many of them in the tourist industry. Other employers include universities, hospitals, banks, call centres and utility services. However although the city has a large number of billionaires, it also has Turkey's highest unemployment rate, and the gap between rich and poor is strikingly visible.

A Grand Bazaar has been located on this site in the Fatih district since 1461, surviving fires and earthquakes over the centuries. The covered market offered security to the city's traders, where their wares could be locked up and guarded by night.

The Kadiköy district on the Asian side of Istanbul is famous for its fresh fish and seafood, with small restaurants and a bustling market.

The skyline of Istanbul's modern business districts towers above the old city and the seashore, a symbol of the nation's rapid economic growth.

Istanbul road workers take a break during the evening rush hour.

Washing is hung out to dry on old houses in Balat, once a poorer district which was home to Jews and Greeks. It is now being restored and is attracting new money.

THE GROWING CITIES

URBAN HOTSPOTS

In ancient times Izmir was known as Smyrna. Industrialisation and massive population increase transformed this city in the later 20th century.

Istanbul and Ankara may be Turkey's top two cities, but many others are growing rapidly. Izmir, on the Aegean coast, has a population of well over three million. Bursa, Adana, Gaziantep, Konya, Anatalya and Kayseri are all big residential or industrial centres, their streets jammed with noisy traffic and thronged with shoppers.

THE URBAN SWITCH

It was not always like this. Back in 1935, over 75 per cent of Turks were still village dwellers. Fast forward to today, and we find that nearly that same proportion of the population is now living in towns and cities. Urbanisation is still increasing by 1.7 per cent each year. It has been caused chiefly by industrial development, as factories and other workplaces offer better, more secure wages and an easier life than working on the land.

Wooden housing in the traditional style can still be seen in corners of Istanbul.

NEIGHBOURHOODS

In traditional Turkish cities there has always been a strong sense of neighbourhood. You can see this in older city districts, often surrounding a mosque. Here you may see wooden housing in the Ottoman style, tiled roofs, projecting upper floors, courtyards, squares, local markets, cafés and alleyways. However modern housing and commercial developments of brick and concrete tend to sprawl out and engulf old neighbourhoods, destroying a sense of community. Critics say that profit now comes before people and heritage. Large numbers of people live in the unplanned sub-standard housing that springs up to cater for the urban poor, or rural migrants seeking work.

SOCIAL IMPACT

As in other rapidly developing countries, urbanisation has helped economic growth, but this has come at a price. Towns have struggled to cope with the flood of people in need of services and affordable housing. Women who previously worked informally on family farms have found it harder to find work in the cities. City life also tends to fragment the wider family connections and networks of support that have always been common in the countryside.

Housing blocks such as these have sprung up across Turkey in recent years.

21

FIELDS AND VILLAGES

FIELDS AND VILLAGES

Olive groves and fields of sunflowers border the Aegean coast. Sheep graze the grasslands of central Anatolia. Cherries and hazelnuts thrive in the Black Sea region of the north, where dairy cattle provide milk and cream. The Turkish landscape is varied, beautiful, and, in the more fertile regions, very productive. Nearly 30 per cent of the land is arable (suitable for agriculture).

Sunflowers have been a major crop since the 1920s, especially in European Turkey. Their seeds are processed to provide vegetable oil.

RURAL COMMUNITIES

Life in small villages is still based on traditions of extended family groupings. However, things are changing. There are more tractors and combine harvesters and fewer labourers in the fields. The removal of farming subsidies by the Erdoğan government has also made many small farmers decide to quit. The tide of rural workers into the cities has become a flood.

Life on the land has often been hard in the past, but in many ways it has now become easier, with better water, electricity supplies and communications. Agriculture still employs over a quarter of Turkey's workforce and brings in about nine per cent of national gross domestic product.

COUNTRY HOME

Housing in Turkey's villages can be made of wood, stone or concrete, with many buildings having white walls and red-tiled roofs. In the Cappadoccia region some traditional housing was carved from rocks and caves – now a popular tourist attraction – and many houses there are still set into the local limestone rock formations.

CROPS AND HARVESTS

Turkey is self-sufficent in farming produce. Turkish farmers grow wheat, rye and barley, as well as root crops such as potatoes and sugarbeet. Tomatoes, cucumbers, aubergines and peppers are also popular crops. The climate is perfect for growing melons, nuts such as almonds and pistachios, and all sorts of fruits from figs, apricots, apples and quinces, to lemons, grapefruit and pomegranates. The olive is native to the region and Turkey is estimated to have about 85 million trees, some of them hundreds of years old. Grapes are cultivated for making wine, and tea plantations provide tea for all those glasses of çay (see page 14). Beehives yield golden, fragrant honey – a common breakfast treat.

Village women collect the potato harvest in the hot Sun.

Ancient rock housing in the Nevşehir province of Central Anatolia.

LAND AND SEA

Turkey produces cotton and wool for its textile industries. Sheep and goats are raised in the plateau, grasslands and mountains, while along the coasts fishing boats bring in tuna, sardines, anchovies and squid.

ON THE MOVE

VITAL LINK

Turkey covers an area over three times
the size of the United Kingdom, and the
journey across Turkey from west to east is
about 1,700 km long. Over the ages the
country's mountainous regions have slowed
down travel and communications. Turkey
has always provided the chief overland route
between Asia and Europe, so good transport
infrastructure is key to future success.

ROAD AND RAIL

Intercity road networks are being improved
in the west. In all, Turkey has some 352,000
km of roads, of which 89 per cent are
paved. Over 2,000 km of roads are of
motorway-standard, mostly toll roads.
Turks own about 15 million vehicles, and
car ownership is growing rapidly. The
main car manufacturers are Ford-Otosan,

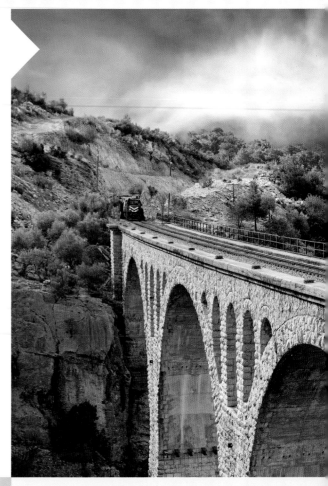

A train crosses the spectacular Varda viaduct in Adana province. This 98-metre high bridge was built by German engineers in 1916.

Long distance trucks queue at a border post. Turkey lies on the overland trading route between Europe and Asian countries such as Iran, Pakistan and India.

Oyak-Renault, Tofaş-Fiat and Toyota.
Coaches provide national services, and city
transport includes buses and taxicabs.
Shared minibus-taxis called *dolmuş* are a way
of life around the cities. They are crowded
and hurtle at speed around city suburbs
– when traffic jams permit.

About 11,000 km of track make up the
TCDD (Turkish State Railways) rail
network, which connects up the Turkish
regions and also takes passengers eastwards
to Iran via a train ferry across Lake Van.
New high-speed rail links are being
constructed in the west to provide a speedier
service between Istanbul and Ankara.

SEA AND AIR

Shipping plays a crucial part in the Turkish economy, and large cargo ships pass under the Bosphorus bridges every day. The major container ports are Haydarpaşa, Ambarlı, Izmir and Mersin. Ferries are also important, carrying local passengers and tourists around Turkey's coasts and lakes. Turkey has 88 airports and external and internal air travel is growing fast. The chief air hub is Atatürk International at Yesilyurt, the largest airport for Istanbul.

A Turkish Airlines Airbus takes off from Istanbul's Atatürk International airport.

The 14 km rail tunnel under the Bosphorus took nine years to build and opened in 2013.

TUNNEL TO THE FUTURE?

About 12 million people now make journeys in and around Istanbul every day. The result of this has been increasing pollution and delay.

- One solution is called the Marmaray project. This involves upgrading suburban rail and rapid transit networks in order to get traffic off the roads. The centrepiece is a new rail tunnel under the Bosphorus strait. Built as a sunken earthquake-proof tube, this is now the deepest tunnel of this type in the world, at one point reaching 60 metres below sea level.

- The project is running four years behind schedule, largely due to the discovery of a huge Byzantine-era archaeological site close to the excavations. It finally opened on 29 October 2013, the 90th anniversary of the founding of the Turkish republic.

AGAINST NATURE?

URBAN HAZE

In cities such as Istanbul, Ankara, Bursa and Erzurum, a hazy smog often hangs in the air. During cold winters the smoke from heating fuels may add to this. The building of new factories, the growth of big cities and the increase in traffic exhaust fumes have all made the air more polluted. Economic development often comes at a high cost to the environment.

Clearing up the beaches after an oil spill. The Black Sea coast has suffered repeatedly from accidents at sea.

As the city of Istanbul spreads outwards, the air becomes polluted and the natural environment is destroyed.

POLLUTION AND DEFORESTATION

Turkey's coasts are at risk of oil spills and pollution, especially at busy shipping bottlenecks such as the straits of the Bosphorus and Dardanelles in northwestern Turkey. The Black Sea, almost enclosed by land, has absorbed industrial, chemical, radioactive and human waste from the surrounding countries. Farmland has seen the over-use of fertilisers, and in many areas there has been over-grazing by herds. Deforestation has also degraded the land, as the removal of tree roots which trap moisture can create a dustbowl. As much as 69 per cent of the country has suffered from soil erosion.

The magnificent Cinereous vulture is endangered due to deforestation and poisoning.

DINNER TIME FOR VULTURES

Vultures are having a hard time worldwide, often poisoned by veterinary chemicals in the dead livestock that they scavenge. Some of Turkey's vulture species are also under threat. In the far east of Anatolia, at Iğdir on the Armenian border, conservationists have created a popular feeding place for the birds, leaving out roadkill, butchers' scraps, or farm animals that have died of natural causes. Hides make it possible for the public to view and photograph these big birds as they feed. Some of the vultures are also being fitted with transmitters so that their migration patterns can be tracked by satellite.

THE ENERGY DEBATE

Fossil fuels such as oil, gas or coal are big polluters, and Turkey uses them to generate 65 per cent of its energy. The government is planning a new nuclear power programme, but a proposed plant at Akkuyu in Mersin province has aroused opposition due to safety concerns. Over 32 per cent of Turkey's energy comes from hydroelectric schemes, but the building of new dams has also been controversial, putting the environment and communities at risk and potentially reducing the water supply to neighbouring Syria, Iraq and Georgia. There are plans to increase wind and geothermal power, with a target of 30 per cent of total energy coming from renewable sources by 2023.

PROTECTING WILDLIFE

There is a lot at stake here. Turkey is on major migration routes for birds and its varied landscapes are a precious world resource. They include forests, steppes, mountains, wetlands, coasts and seas. These ecosystems support a diverse range of plants and animals, and include brown bears, wolves, lynxes and many other creatures which are at risk from hunting as well as loss of habitat. Attempts to improve wildlife conservation are up against relaxed planning laws which were designed to encourage mining or the building of tourist resorts.

SEEKING JUSTICE

HUMAN RIGHTS

All countries in the world are increasingly audited for their human rights record. Criticisms of social justice in Turkey have been raised at many points in its history. Turkey has had to meet various conditions as a result of its application for EU membership and this has brought about improvements. Even so, the United Nations and watchdogs such as Amnesty International and Human Rights Watch still raise concerns. There are accusations of laws not being enforced and a lack of accountability. Victims of injustice have included refugees, asylum seekers, gays, migrant workers and the poor.

TAKSIM SUMMER

In May 2013 a public protest in Istanbul's Taksim Gezi Park dominated news headlines around the world. It started with a small protest about urban development, but soon turned into a major occupation of the district and spread to other cities. There was a confrontation between the protestors on one side and the police and Prime Minister Erdoğan on the other. The issues in dispute included the right of assembly, press freedom, free speech and the protection of Turkey's secular constitution. Protestors were treated harshly. The extent of opposition to Erdoğan's authority was now clear. Was he losing touch?

The protestors in Istanbul were made up of many different factions, united against a number of different government policies.

CEYLAN'S STORY

Turkish women won the vote in the 1930s and the first female prime minister, Tansu Çiller, was elected in 1993. Women are prominent in public life. However, all is not well. Violence against women is widespread, in modern city homes as well as in remote rural areas. In some regions there are so-called 'honour killings', in which women who marry against the wishes of their parents are killed by their own family or forced to commit suicide. The case of Ceylan Sosyal, a 19-year-old woman from Hatay province, shocked Turkey in 2011. After an unapproved marriage, Ceylan's new husband abandoned her and she was then murdered by her brother. This tragedy has resulted in vocal campaigns against violence towards women. In 2013 Turkey's parliamentary Constitution Commission added guarantees of protection against domestic violence, early and forced marriage.

LAW AND ORDER

The Turkish police is the chief agency for law enforcement, and blue-and-white police uniforms and patrol cars are a familiar sight on city streets. The gendarmerie, a military trained body, carries out most rural policing. Turkey's legal system is influenced by various European models. It is based on the 1982 constitution and was reformed in 1991 and 2004. Judges are independent from the government. There are civil and criminal courts, and also separate courts for military, constitutional and state security matters. The latter often attract political controversy, dealing with organised crime, terrorism and sedition. Jail conditions have been criticised by human rights organisations, but no death sentences have been passed since 2004.

The number of prisoners in Turkey more than doubled between 2004 and 2013.

Ceylan Sosyal, victim of a horrific 'honour killing'.

HEALTH AND EDUCATION

STARTING SCHOOL

At about 8.15 each morning, children line up in rows, before filing into the schoolroom under a portrait of Kemal Atatürk. As the founder of the modern Turkish republic, he was the first to bring a rational – and national – approach to education in Turkey. Since then the period in which children have to attend school has been extended from five to eight years, and again to 12 years, between the ages of six and 18. Schooling is divided into three stages – four years at primary (first level), four years at primary (second level) and four years at secondary. In addition, children may have pre-school education or go on to study at college or university.

WHAT KIND OF EDUCATION?

Teachers in Turkey have always taught pupils to learn things off by heart. Now a new curriculum plans to place children at the centre of the learning process. However there may be a need for better funding to bring real change. Turkey currently spends 3.7 per cent of its GDP on education – much the same as Russia, for example, but lower than most EU countries. The education system is run by the state, but there are also some private schools. Almost all men (95 per cent) can read and write, but just under 80 per cent of women are literate. In some rural areas it is still difficult to get families to send their girls to school.

A teacher helps children with their class work. Secondary pupils have six lessons lasting 40 minutes each school day.

PUBLIC HEALTH

How long can you expect to live? In Turkey the average figures are nearly 71 years for a male and 75 for a female. Common health problems include cancer, heart disease, stroke and infectious diseases. In recent years, the improvement of water supplies and a public smoking ban show that practical steps are being taken towards improvements in public health. Turkey has 1.5 doctors and 2.4 hospital beds per 1,000 of the population. These statistics compare with 2.7 and 3.4 respectively in the UK. A growing number of overseas visitors come to Turkey for medical treatment. Since 2003 Erdoğan has set about privatising the state healthcare system. His reforms have been welcomed by some, but have also attracted criticism and protests.

A hospital nurse hands a new-born baby over to its happy mother. Home births are more common in rural areas.

More than 6 per cent of the Turkish population are over 65 years old.

MEDIA TALK

CHANGING TIMES

The Turkish communications media, as elsewhere, are going through a period of rapid change. In the old days, the press was dominated by big press corporations, who had close relations with the government and the military and supported their agenda. In recent years large sections of the media have been bought up by business leaders who sympathise with the privatising programme of the Erdoğan government.

Readers have a wide range of newspapers to choose from, from the conservative Zaman *to the more left-wing* Posta.

SATELLITE DISHES

Television reaches about 18 million Turkish households these days, and satellite dishes beam in a multitude of channels. TRT still has a large share of the TV and radio audience, and has at last provided a Kurdish-language service as well. There is growing interest in Turkish-made programmes rather than imports. Even these can cause political upset. In 2012 a popular costume drama serial called *Muhteşem Yüzyıl* (*Magnificent Century*) was fiercely attacked by Prime Minister Erdoğan for its portrayal of the most famous Ottoman sultan, Suleiman the Magnificent.

FREE TO HAVE YOUR SAY?

Journalists, bloggers and Internet users have found that discussing certain topics can be dangerous. Sensitive subjects can include ideas that conservatives might label as 'anti-Turkish', such as the legacy of Atatürk, the Kurdish question, religious issues, the role of the military and radical activism. In 2013 the pianist and composer Fazıl Say, an outspoken critic of the Erdoğan government, was given a 10-month suspended jail term for having mocked certain religious practices on Twitter. It was estimated in 2013 that Turkey had more journalists in prison than any other country in the world.

Traditional housing, new media. Satellite dishes decorate the rooftops of Ankara.

Mobile phone usage in Turkey is increasing fast, among old and young alike.

INTERNET ACCESS

The new communications media are overturning tradition, changing society and raising all sorts of questions about rights and freedoms. Turkey has about 15.2 million land lines and 65 million mobile phones. As of 2012 there were 35 million Internet users. There is a big take-up of the main social media networks, such as Facebook. The government has been censoring the Internet for some years and blocking websites of which it disapproves, on political as well as moral grounds. That is a familiar story around the world, but new media is much harder to control than older forms.

ARTS, LEISURE AND SPORT

TURKISH ROOTS

The Turkish music tradition is very different from that of Western Europe, although over the centuries there has always been interchange with European and Middle Eastern cultures. It has its origins in the Ottoman court, in religious and military music, in dancing and folk traditions. The literature, arts and crafts of the Ottoman world are still celebrated. Examples include beautiful poetry, breathtaking architecture, art in miniature and elegant calligraphy (handwriting art), precious inlaid woods, dazzling metal work, embroidered textiles and patterned pottery and tiles from the town of Iznik.

SOUND AND VISION

Many traditional influences and themes filter into contemporary music and arts scenes. Mainstream pop in Turkey has had offshoots from Anatolian rock to hip-hop and metal, and in some cases there is fusion with folk roots. Turkey has made its mark on the international art scene too. Since the Istanbul Biennial show was set up in 1988, exciting new galleries have been opening up all over the city, exhibiting art that is often striking, irreverent and witty. Today's best known Turkish writers include Nobel Prize winner Orhan Pamuk (b.1952) and Elif Şafak (b.1971), a writer who is inspired not only by political change and the equality of women, but also by Turkey's long history of poetry and mysticism.

A rug is handwoven in the town of Göreme. Turkey has been known for its carpets and rugs for about 9,000 years.

Once Upon a Time in Anatolia is just one of Turkish cinema's recent success stories.

MAKING MOVIES

Turkish cinema dates back to 1914 and was very popular from the 1950s to the 1970s. Today there is a revival and Turkey produces more films than any European country other than France. Some Turkish film makers are highly respected. Director Semih Kaplanoglu's *Bal* picked up the Berlin Film Festival's Golden Bear in 2010, while Nuri Bilge Ceylan's *Bir Zamaniar Anadolu'da (Once Upon a Time in Anatolia)* jointly won top prize at the Cannes Film Festival in 2011.

Galatasaray fans celebrate a goal during an away game in the Champions League competition.

SPORTING ARENAS

Turkish weightlifters and wrestlers often perform impressively in international competitions. Wrestling by competitors smeared in olive oil is one of Turkey's traditional sports, with its own rules and festivals. The big spectator sport in Turkey is football. There are five professional leagues, one of which is for women. Top clubs, famous across Europe, include Fenerbahçe, Beşiktaş and Galatasaray (who are said to have the loudest fans in the world!).

FAITH AND FESTIVALS

A MUSLIM LAND

Islam is the prevailing religion in Turkey. The Islamic faith proclaims that there is one God (Allah *pbuh*) and that Muhammad is his prophet. Muslims must believe, pray five times daily, give charitably, fast during the month known in Turkish as Ramazan, and make a pilgrimage to Mecca (in Saudi Arabia). It has been claimed that 98 per cent of all Turks are Muslim, but numbers and definitions are hard to pin down. Around eight out of ten Turkish Muslims follow the mainstream Sunni branch of the faith. Others are known as Alevi and follow an ancient Anatolian tradition. Alevism includes elements of the Shi'a branch of Islam, but it remains independent. Some declare that it is outside Islam altogether, as Alevi do not follow normal Muslim practices.

Friends in Istanbul gather before the start of the Islamic holy month of Ramazan. For the next month they will not eat or drink during the hours of daylight.

The Christian church of the Holy Cross was built in 921 CE by the Armenian Apostolic Church. It is located on an island in Lake Van, in Eastern Turkey.

OTHER RELIGIONS

There are very small religious minorities in Turkey, including Jews and Christians belonging to various eastern and western traditions. They have been tolerated for hundreds of years. Of these only Jews, Armenian and Greek Orthodox Christians have official recognition, and the Turkish constitution remains secular.

WHIRLING MYSTICS

Alevi beliefs chime with those of Sufism, a mystical practice in Islam. Mysticism in any religion is a way of approaching God through personal meditation or spiritual exercises. A Turkish Sufi order called the Mevlevi, based in the city of Konya, achieve a trance-like state by performing a dance to chanting and the music of drums and flute. They whirl round and round in ecstasy, wearing white robes and tall hats which symbolise human mortality. This ritual was founded by Rumi, a great Persian poet of the 1200s, and may still be seen today.

IN CELEBRATION

Festivals mark the Turkish religious year. The end of the Islamic fasting period of Ramazan is called Şeker Bayramı (sugar feast) and is marked by three days of holiday, the giving of sweets, new clothes, shadow puppet shows and visits to relatives. Secular holidays include New Year's Eve, which is celebrated with public firework displays, street performances and parties. The founding of the Grand National Assembly is commemorated on 23 April, a date which is also celebrated as International Children's Day, with dancing, concerts and sporting events. Republic Day (29 October) is the time for parades, flags, marching bands – and more fireworks.

The Sema or ritual dance of the Mevlevi is a remarkable form of religious experience.

FOCUS ON: ISTANBUL

ENJOY THE CITY!

There's one peaceful way to escape the hustle and bustle of Istanbul – sea angling from the bridges or waterfront on a lazy sunny day. Old men can chat with their friends and bring home fresh grilled mackerel (*istravit*) for dinner too.

FEASTING

Eating is a pleasure in this city, and meals are often served outdoors. Aubergines, peppers, olives, sheep's cheese, yoghurt, mint and rice are all common ingredients. There are tasty snacks such as vine leaves wrapped around rice, and *hummus*, a chickpea paste. Then there are soups, fresh seafood such as octopus or shrimps, meatballs, lamb or chicken kebabs. For a sweet tooth, there is *baklava* (pastries made with honey and pistachio), *halva* (crushed sesame seeds), *lokum* (jellies flavoured with rosewater and nuts, known around the world as 'Turkish delight') and Istanbul's delicious milk and rice puddings.

CUP OF COFFEE?

Istanbul invented the coffee shop, with the public sale of coffee first recorded here as early as 1475. The Turkish version is brewed in a long-handled copper pot called an *ibrik*. It is served strong and thick, and often drunk sweet, accompanied by a glass of cold water.

BATH TIME

For those in search of a healthier lifestyle, a visit to a traditional *hamam* or Turkish bath may be called for. Public baths have been a part of city life here for thousands of years, offering combinations of hot and cold air and water and a vigorous massage with oil or soap.

FOOTBALL FANS

Sports fans ran riot in the ancient city of Constantinople, battling over top teams in the chariot races at the Hippodrome. Today football is the city's main sporting passion, with local club Fenerbahçe as the stars. The city has four major stadiums and arenas.

ARTS AND CULTURE

Istanbul was declared Europe's 'Capital of Culture' for 2010 and at any time it has rich cultural offerings, from the dazzling displays of Ottoman history in the Topkapi Palace to shows of cutting edge art at Istanbul Modern – the city's museum of modern art.

Spectacular fireworks light up the Bosphorus in celebration of Republic Day (29 October), a public holiday.

A fashionable dining spot in the Beyoğlu district offers fine views of the city and the Bosphorus.

The splendid Cağaloğlu Turkish baths were built in 1741 by Sultan Mahmud I, and are still open for use today.

As long as there are fish swimming in the Golden Horn, Istanbul's anglers will be standing on Galata Bridge to catch them.

TURKEY AND THE WORLD

AROUND THE WORLD

Turks do not just live in Turkey. Turkish communities are scattered around the globe, which creates useful connections with other nations, markets and cultures. Over five million live in Western Europe, in particular in Germany and the Netherlands, where they were recruited as foreign workers from the 1960s onwards. There are also many Turks living in the Middle East and North America.

CYPRUS

The island of Cyprus has both Greek and Turkish populations and this has led to 50 years of ethnic rivalry and division. Northern Cyprus declared its independence as a separate Turkish state in 1974 and Turkey invaded in support. This mini-state has never been recognised internationally.

ALLIANCES

Turkey has remained a member of NATO, and its geographical position between Europe, Russia and the Middle East makes it a crucial ally of Western governments. Turkey is in the Council of Europe and is an associate member of the EU. It applied for full membership in 2005. This is a slow process, but it has been delayed further by concerns within the EU about enlargement of the union. Turkey's European supporters say it would be a valuable addition, a bridge to the Middle East. Economic problems across Europe have also caused concern on all sides. However the application alone has already had one result, encouraging democratic reform in Turkey.

Young Turks at this school in Duisburg, Germany, receive religious education in the Alevi tradition.

Israel has long been one of Turkey's regional allies. Relations were set back in 2010 by an Israeli attack on a ship carrying Turkish citizens protesting about Israeli actions in Gaza.

FLASHPOINTS

The lands to the east and south of Turkey have been in a state of political turmoil for many decades. Iran has seen great political and religious upheavals, as has Iraq, torn apart by years of war. Kurdish rebellions have spilt across the borders. Turkey's relations with the former lands of the Ottoman empire, such as Egypt, are still very important. Prime minister Erdoğan may hope that a powerful and economically successful Turkey may regain a wider regional influence.

SYRIA

Since 2010 a wave of protests, uprisings and civil wars have flared up across the Arab world. In 2011 this 'Arab Spring' reached Syria, Turkey's southern neighbour. Protests against the regime of Bashar al-Assad soon developed into a terrible conflict, with many Syrian and international factions fighting the government. There have been clashes across the Turkish border, with a Turkish jet being shot down and five Turks killed by Syrian army shellfire. Turkey has provided support to the rebels and over 400,000 Syrians have fled into Turkey, to be housed in 15 refugee camps.

Refugees from the fighting in Syria camp at Reyhanlı on the Turkish side of the border.

FACING THE FUTURE

SPECIAL CELEBRATION

Weddings are important affairs in Turkey, preceded by meetings between the two families and the exchange of gifts. All sorts of traditional customs may be honoured, such as the decoration of the bride's hands with henna and the wearing of a red ribbon, a symbol of virginity. There may be a wedding procession, the exchange of gifts, dancing, singing and feasting. Celebrations can go on for days.

A PAUSE FOR THOUGHT

Whether the wedding is a traditional village gathering or a sophisticated city affair, it offers a chance for families to consider the past and look to the future. Most Turkish couples marry between the age of 17 and their early 20s, so they will themselves have been part of the great changes which their country has gone through in recent years. If they are fortunate their family may have prospered from the economic upturn. If not, they may be struggling to pay their way.

IMPORTANT QUESTIONS

What kind of future can today's young Turkish people expect for their own children? Can economic development be sustained? Will there be more or less equality between men and women, Turk and Kurd? Will human rights and democratic values be respected? Will society be secular or religious? Today's young people belong to the generation that will need to help decide these questions.

Just married! What does the future hold for these young Turkish people?

A TIME FOR HOPE

The view of Turkey as a bridge between western and eastern values is nothing new. This role has been a fact of life for thousands of years. Modern Europeans and Asians need to respect this tradition and encourage it, in their own interest. But of course Turkey is more than just a bridge or a conduit. It is a remarkable nation in its own right, with a rich history and culture and a people known to be hardy and tough, talented and hospitable. All of these are factors which should give newly-weds hope for their children's future. As an old Turkish proverb says *'Çikmayan candan ümit kesilmez.'* Its closest English equivalent? 'As long as there is life, there is hope.'

These refugees are Turkish Kurds who fled over the border in the 1990s. The peace process of 2013 at last gives them hope of one day returning home.

Sweeping plains and eroded rock formations – the backdrop of the new Turkey is a very ancient landscape.

GLOSSARY

Alevi a Turkish religious group which combines various Islamic traditions such as Sufism and some Shi'a beliefs

arable describing land that is suitable for growing crops

bazaar a market or shopping district. The Turkish word is *çarşı*

Byzantine Empire an empire which grew out of the Roman empire and lasted until 1453. It was largely Greek-speaking and its capital was Constantinople (today's Istanbul)

calligraphy writing as a form of art

communist believing that the workers, or a party representing them, should be in charge of political and economic activity within a state

Constantinople a city founded by the Romans in 330 CE on the site of ancient Byzantium

constitution the laws, rules and principles by which a country is governed

curriculum the programme of learning within a school

deforestation The loss or destruction of forest and woodland

democracy government by the people or by their representatives, rather than by a dictator or monarch

ecosystem an interactive community of living things within a particular environment

ethnic group people who share common descent, culture, customs or language

ethnic Turk someone of the Turkish ethnic group

executive powers having the authority to run the country

fossil fuel any carbon-based fuel such as coal, gas or oil

free market an economic system based on supply and demand, with little government control

gendarmerie A type of police force or militia

GDP Gross Domestic Product a measure of wealth within a nation, region or city, often defined by the total amount spent on goods and services

gecekondu a Turkish word meaning poor, makeshift housing that can be built overnight

genocide the systematic extermination of a national or ethnic group

geothermal energy energy obtained from the inner heat of the Earth

honour killing the murder of a family member who is believed to have bought shame on the family

human rights a human's essential requirements for justice and equality

Kemalism a Turkish political movement based on the ideas of Mustafa Kemal Atatürk

manufacturing making raw materials into a finished product, as in a factory process

minaret a tall, slender spire on a mosque, used for calling Muslims to prayer

minority a smaller group within a larger one, such as a small ethnic group within a nation

mysticism seeking a direct consciousness of God, often through ritual or meditation

nationalist (1) supporting the creation of an independent or liberated nation; (2) believing in the superiority of one's own nation (ultra-nationalism)

Ottoman (1) a branch of the Turkish people originally ruled by Osman I. (2) the name given to the Turks of Turkey and the empire they created

privatisation handing over state-run enterprises to private companies

reprisal retaliation

republic a country with an elected head of state and government

rural in the countryside

secular non-religious

sedition stirring up opposition to a government

Seljuks a Turkish people who moved into the Middle East and conquered parts of the Byzantine empire in the Middle Ages

service industries industries which do not make things but provide services, such as banking, tourism or catering

strait a channel, a narrow strip of sea

sultan a Muslim king or emperor

sunken tube tunnel a tunnel that is not bored, but made from a tube lowered from the surface

Turkic related to the wider groupings of Turks and their languages

urbanisation the growth of towns and cities

FURTHER INFORMATION

BOOKS

Countries of the World: Turkey, Sarah Shields (National Geographic, 2009)

The Middle East, Philip Steele (Kingfisher Books, 2009)

WEBSITES

http://www.timemaps.com/ history/turkey-1500bc
See the map of Turkey change through the ages, from ancient times to the 21st century.

http://travel.nationalgeographic. co.uk/travel/countries/ turkey-facts/
A simple summary of facts about Turkey.

http://en.wikipedia.org/wiki/ Timeline_of_Turkish_history
This timeline runs through a detailed history of Turkey from the 11th century.

http://www.turkish-football.com/
Turkey for football fans.

Every effort has been made by the Publishers to ensure that the websites in this book are suitable for children, and that they contain no inappropriate or offensive material. However, because of the nature of the Internet, it is impossible to guarantee that the contents of these sites will not be altered. We strongly advise that Internet access is supervised by a responsible adult.

INDEX